The Musical Barn

by David Siegel
illustrated by Liisa Chauncy Guida

Harcourt
SCHOOL PUBLISHERS

Requests for permission to make copies of any part of the work should be addressed to School Permissions and Copyrights, Harcourt, Inc., 6277 Sea Harbor Drive, Orlando, Florida 32887-6777. Fax: 407-345-2418.

HARCOURT and the Harcourt Logo are trademarks of Harcourt, Inc., registered in the United States of America and/or other jurisdictions.

Printed in China

ISBN 10: 0-15-350503-6
ISBN 13: 978-0-15-350503-4

Ordering Options
ISBN 10: 0-15-350333-5 (Grade 3 Below-Level Collection)
ISBN 13: 978-0-15-350333-7 (Grade 3 Below-Level Collection)
ISBN 10: 0-15-357491-7 (package of 5)
ISBN 13: 978-0-15-357491-7 (package of 5)

2 3 4 5 6 7 8 9 10 985 12 11 10 09 08 07

Every morning, when the sun is about to rise on Arkady's farm, the first one to notice is the rooster. His loud crow rings like an alarm clock. The farm animals that have been sedentary all night wake up. They yawn and stretch. Then the pig, mouse, horse, ducks, and chickens all get busy.

As the sun rises higher in the sky, the ducks go down to the pond. You can hear them boasting, "I caught the most fish," or "I can swim the fastest."

If you are inside the barn, you can see the sun shine through the windows. It lights up every dim corner.

Look hard into those corners. Do you see? There are three spider webs.

All through their long history, spiders have built webs. Building webs is never a nuisance for a spider because in its web, it catches its dinner.

The spiders in this barn spin a special
kind of web. Each of the webs makes
beautiful music.

Every morning, a spider named Mem
runs outside. She gathers drops of dew,
and then she sprinkles her web with these
tiny droplets of water. When the wind blows
through Mem's web, the strands of dew
sound like wind chimes.

Bill, another spider, hangs dried corn on strands of his web. Then he jiggles the web. The action of the strands makes the corn click and rub together so that Bill's web sounds like a little drum.

Jan's web is the largest web. It is very near a window. When the window is open, air blows through the strands. The wind strums the strands, and the web sounds like a harp.

The spiders like to play music together. They hold practice sessions and give concerts.

Today there is so much wind that
the harp-web sounds grand. The corn
clicks a loud beat. The dewdrops chime
a pretty melody.

Presto the Mouse and Hoggins the Pig
think the tune is just right for dancing.
Presto dances and jumps, while Hoggins
wiggles and spins.

9

Presto jumps higher and higher. Oh, no! Presto has jumped too high, and he is stuck in Jan's huge web! What a commotion! Hoggins squeals, summoning all the animals to come and help Presto. All of the animals oblige and come running to see what can be done.

All morning, the spiders and farm animals talk and think. They argue about the best way to help Presto.

Then Hoggins has a fantastic idea! He sends the spiders to fetch some of his best food scraps. The spiders work together.

Then the spiders carry the food up to Presto, and Presto eats and eats and eats. Soon his very full stomach begins to weigh him down, and he begins to sway. Presto has eaten so much that he falls off the web and lands right in the middle of a heap of scraps.

Presto is free, and Jan's web is safe.
The spiders look it over, and they see
that there is no harm done. What a relief!
"The best thing to do with all those
happy feelings," declares Mem, "is to
play music!"

As the sun begins to set, Presto digs
through the lovely scraps. He finds an
apple peel and picks it up. "Dessert," he
sighs happily. Hoggins joins him, and the
animals all dine and play and dance into
the night.

Think Critically

1. When does the story begin? When does it end?

2. How are the spider webs in this story different from spider webs you know about?

3. How can you tell that Hoggins and Presto are friends?

4. Which parts of this story could not happen in real life? Which parts could happen in real life?

5. Was Hoggins the Pig's plan a good one? Explain.

 Science

Web Work Find a picture of a spider web in a book. Create your own web with a finely sharpened pencil, and then draw in some spiders so that they will have a new home.

School-Home Connection Different things happen throughout the day on the farm in this story. Make a chart of your daily schedule.

Word Count: 561